Ghosts of Old Rochesterville

Ghosts of Old Rochesterville

Ralph Esposito

In Loving Memory of My Parents

Contents

Preface

Who doesn't like a good ghost story? Like many people, I began my interest in ghosts at a young age watching B&W horror movies on Saturdays, then, reading novels of ghosts and haunted houses as I got older. This awakened an interest in the paranormal that has stayed with me to this day.

Then of course there's that life after death curiosity. Who isn't interested, at least the tiny bit, in the afterlife? It is a question we all have whether you are strong in faith, or an atheist.

I began to get seriously interested in ghost hunting in 2003. An opportunity opened to join a group of like minded folks in my area. We began regular meetings and shared our ghostly experiences. Well, at that time I had never really had any ghostly experiences, but was fascinated by their stories.

Our little group planned a few hunts, starting with local cemeteries and parks. Many parks have quite an interesting history behind them, haunted history as well. Several of the stories are from those early ghost hunts.

The group picked up more members, and eventually ended up at Rolling Hills Mall, the old Genesee County Poor House. It's quite haunted; it has been featured on one of the episodes of Ghost Hunters on the Sci-Fi Channel. Part of the original group currently helps to conduct the Rolling Hills overnight ghost hunts in the mall.

In 2004 I formed a business called Rochester Candle Light Ghost Walks, with a fellow ghost hunter Jenni Lynn. We began doing ghost walks in the Rochester Area and **Ghost Tales and Dinner at a Haunted Pub** presentations at a local restaurant. Currently we do these only in October or by appointment the rest of the year. I enjoy doing them immensely, they are fun, and many times I learn from the guests.

In 2006 an opportunity to do a cable access show on ghosts hunting came up. We called it **Mystic Encounters**, and it has aired around Monroe County. It's a lot of fun and we have had a positive response from viewers. We are looking forward to a 2008 season.

By this time I had been collecting ghost stories from many sources. Most are the small stories that would have been forgotten in a generation. I found the stories interesting, some funny and some very touching. They are stories that I felt should be told. I hope you enjoy them.

7 - Ghosts of Old Rochesterville

Acknowledgements

I would like to thank the many people who in both large and small ways helped me with this project. First, I want to mention all the kind people who shared their wonderful stories with me. It's not always easy to tell about your encounter with a ghost.

I want to say a special thank you to all the friends who encouraged and helped me write this book. Especially Frank, Shelly, Gail and the gang I go ghost hunting with. Each with their unique talents that helped me gather stories, write, polish and publish them.

And finally, Kathy Wilkins: she is a teacher, artist, and musician. Not only did Kathy do the art work for this book, more importantly she attempted to teach me the proper use of a comma. Some of it actually stuck! She proof - read my stories and helped release my creativity to add details and improve my writing. She deserves a medal for all the time she spent helping me with grammar and the stories.

Introduction

The local history of the Rochester area is steeped in a rich and somewhat bloody history. It dates back to the mid 1600's when the French first set foot ashore in Irondequoit. There were wars for greed, conquest, territory, and independence fought over this area.

Rochesterville was formed in 1817, and eventually it swallowed up a number of nearby settlements and several ports. It grew to be renamed Rochester, a major metropolitan area.

With any book on ghosts it would be remiss not to mention Rochester New York as the nexus of the Spiritualist movement. The three Fox Sisters who lived in Hydesville, a small town east of Rochester, claimed to have communicated with the ghost of a dead peddler through a code using knocks. He had been murdered and buried in the basement of their home years prior to their family buying the house. In the mid 1800's the Fox Sisters became celebrated mediums, in Rochester, and throughout both the United States and Europe. They would conduct public meetings, where they would contact the spirits. This was the beginning of the Spiritualism movement.

As you read this book you may ask "Is a ghost story truth or fiction?" That's a very good question. All the stories in this book are from either my own experiences, or were told to me by people on one of my investigations or ghost walks. They experienced the "ghost" first hand. In most stories, I changed the names of the living and give only the street name, to respect the privacy of the families.

To check the accuracy of some of the stories I went to the actual location, with a medium that was told nothing of the stories. The medium was asked her impressions from each location. The amazing thing is how close the medium's impressions were to the stories. In addition, I went to local historians in order to verify the names and other bits of the stories.

I am not going to tell you ghosts are real. That is for you to decide for yourself; as for me, my money is on the ghosts. One thing I have found, there are a lot of ghost stories out there. Most are not legend status like "The White Lady of Durand Eastman Park," those are the ones everyone hears about. These are the small ones, ones that still deserve to be told and remembered. That is, if you like ghost stories…

13 - Ghosts of Old Rochesterville

The Lost City of Tryon

The Lost City of Tryon. Sounds like a movie title. In it, an old adventurer like Errol Flynn swings his machete at the thick green leaves. The heavy leaves fall away to reveal the legendary lost city of Tryon!

The real city of Tryon was never lost nor was it ever a city. It was a gamble that was lost, overtaken by Clinton's Ditch.

Back in 1799, John Tryon purchased the land around what was called Indian Landing, now Ellison Park in Monroe County, NY. Irondequoit Creek at that time was both wider and deeper; Indian Landing was the spot where cargo schooners could dock.

It got its name because it was a convenient place to trade with the local Indians.

An historic marker relates some of the area's history:

"The most important place in the early history of the Genesee Country, all of whose trails led to Irondequoit Bay. A gateway of the Iroquois Confederacy. Here were scenes of adventure and romance for more than 300 years, involving Indian wars, the struggle for empire between the French and English and the Revolutionary and pioneer period. Religion, commerce and war made this territory a famous battleground, bringing here many noted traders, priests and soldiers."

From the Marquee Denville marching through the area in 1687 in a war to wipe out the Seneca Indians, to the settlers coming in the 1800's, the ground of Western NY is steeped in blood, ambition, and history. Such famous units as Rogers Rangers tread the same paths that are today used by hikers, joggers and others.

It was a time of big ideas and a vast wilderness in which to build them. The year 1799, a man named John Tryon purchased the land around Indian Landing. In Tryon's time goods and people came either overland or by boat and Indian landing was a port on Irondequoit Creek. Tryon wanted to build a town around that landing and call it Tryon City.

Soon Tryon City had a dry goods store, blacksmith's shop, shoe factory, distillery, tavern, tannery, large gristmill, ship yard, school, warehouses and cemetery.

John Tryon died in 1808 and that was a serious blow to Tryon City. Tryon had never attracted a large number of residents and with the building of the Erie Canal that bypassed Tryon City for Rochesterville much of the trade began to fall off. By 1923 Rochesterville was drawing more and more business, and became known as Rochester, and Tryon City was all but abandoned.

Eventually Tryon City was swallowed up by the growing city of Rochester and became what is now Ellison Park. All that is left of the settlement are a couple of markers, an old log cabin replica trading post where Fort Schuyler once stood, and one of the original homes built by the settlers.

While the memory of Indian Landing and Tryon City is almost gone (it is all but a few lines in the history books) it seems some of the original residents are more determined not to be forgotten.

By day it is a lovely area, a lazy creek winding through parkland. By night a stranger feeling is prevalent. The ghosts of the area, Native Americans, pioneers, military all died trying to tame the area. I will tell you of two specters I met one evening.

My friend Shelly, a very gifted psychic, enjoys ghost hunting. I was curious to see what she would pick up in the park. I had been there several times before with another ghost hunting group and there seemed to be lots of activity.

We parked and before we got out of the car Shelly was aware of a ghost nearby. He walked up to her dressed in a blue military uniform with a sergeant's insignia. While I could not see him, the hair on my arms was standing on end. She said he was looking at us wondering about our strange conveyance.

Shelly said he seemed a little confused and agitated as he told us our lives were in mortal danger as the Indians are waiting to ambush anyone who went down the path.

He began to tell her what had happened to his patrol. He was leading a patrol to the nearby hill so they could watch the area. As they quietly walked the trail the Indians attacked from the heavy undergrowth. He winced in pain as an arrow tore into his shoulder and he slowly fell forward watching in horror as many of his men fell also. After the first flight of arrows, the warriors attacked hand to hand with tomahawks and war clubs. The brave patrol fought just as savagely against its attackers who had the advantage in numbers. They killed several warriors, wounding others as they fell one by one to the last man.

When the short but bloody ambush was over, the warriors checked the soldiers to make sure they were all dead. They quickly dispatched any survivors with a crushing blow from a war club. The sergeant, weak from his wound closed his eyes and feigned death, silently praying they would miss him. As the Indians left, he staggered up and headed back to report.

The sergeant thought his feint had worked and didn't realize the Indians had not been fooled; his lifeless body lay with his men on that path so many years ago. His last thoughts were that he must get back to report what happened and give warning. He also wanted to be sure his men's bodies were recovered and given a proper burial.

Now he wanders the path telling anyone who will listen to go back, that hostile Indians are nearby waiting to ambush anyone on the trail. As for his being a bit confused, well, getting hit with a war club might confuse the best of us.

I stood there listening to Shelly talk with the ghost when I felt a sensation like a soft hand touching my hair.

"Shelly..." I whispered.

When Shelly looked over she chuckled and said "I see one found you too."

It was an oddly soothing feeling. She told me she saw the spirit of a young Indian girl stroking my hair and softly speaking to me. Her words I could not hear but her gentle fingers were another matter entirely. She was attracted by my hair; Shelly said it was like her husband's. She was searching for him and hoped I might know where her husband was.

Early one morning her husband had set out from the village for the place the white men called Indian Landing. He was hoping to trade some of his handcrafted jewelry with the white traders at the landing. He hoped to get a new knife and several other items for the jewelry.

Another brave was to go with him that morning but his friend was not able. There was always a danger of going alone through the woods as occasionally small groups of Huron would come into the Seneca's land to raid and plunder. The Huron were the enemy of the Seneca.

He had no problems getting to Indian Landing. The jewelry fetched a nice trade: the new knife he had wanted, an iron pot for his wife and several other metal goods. It was time to return home. He was alone on the trail about an hour from the Landing when out of the underbrush four Huron braves jumped out surrounding him.   They fell upon him and though he struggled valiantly they quickly overpowered and killed him. They dragged his body off the trail. The Hurons divided up the trade goods he had received, then hid his body so it would be difficult to find. It would give them more time without alerting the Seneca that they were there.

When her husband did not return, the tribe sent out a group of braves to search for him. They came back with no news, only that he had made it to Indian Landing and traded with the white traders there. Though suspicious, they had found no sign of the ambush.

His wife cried and mourned the loss of her husband. Today she still searches for him at the Indian Landing where he was last seen. If you feel a soft hand touching your hair while playing Frisbee golf at Ellison Park perhaps it is his widow still looking for her husband – remembering the hair of her beloved husband that she longs to touch again.

We left shortly after that wondering how many other stories lie in the lost city of Tryon.

21 - Ghosts of Old Rochesterville

The Barmaid

I met my psychic friend Shelly one evening for coffee, and our conversation led to an interesting ghostly adventure. She mentioned that where she worked, lurking in the basement was a ghost... a ghost who wanted her story told.

For a week Shelly was being bothered by uncomfortable feelings at work. It was as if someone was close to her neck and left shoulder. The feelings were more intense when she was in the basement. In addition, every so often the scale next to her desk would bounce up and down as if an unseen hand slapped it.

She invited me to stop by and see what I could find. I use pendulums and divining rods to "talk" to ghosts and spirits. At dinner break we would chat with the ghost. During this time Shelly was becoming more aware of her psychic abilities and how to use them.

The building in which Shelly works in was a part of the brick works back in the 1800's, near what is now Twelve Corners in Brighton, NY. We communicated with a female ghost who said her name was Miriam. Over the course of several evenings she communicated her story to us.

Miriam was a young woman who worked as a barmaid at the Inn across the street from the brickworks in the mid 1800's, on what is now Monroe Ave. It was a busy place when the brick factory workers stopped by for a drink at the end of the day. She was an only child and her family needed the extra money. She worked long hours helping to support her family, despite the fact that it was not a job that was looked on favorably by polite society. Her one real regret was that it left her little time to find a husband, as most women had done by her age. The tavern was hardly a place to meet a husband with any promise.

Besides Miriam and another barmaid, there was the Inn keeper and a Black busboy who also worked there. He was a big, powerful young man with, large rough hands; and though he seemed respectful enough he liked to watch her and the other barmaid when he thought no one was looking.

The Inn was smoky, gritty, and filled with dirty glasses and dishes as the last of the customers left about midnight. Miriam and the busboy had to clean up the bar before they were finished. She had already caught him leering at her; he quickly averted his eyes and continued working. She knew he looked at her all the time, but tonight the way he looked was enough to make her feel slightly unsettled. Shaking the feeling off, she continued cleaning and thinking how good it would feel to get home.

It was nearing one o'clock and Miriam decided it was time to leave; she could finish the rest of the cleaning in the morning. The busboy took a break out back.

She collected her purse and wrap, then said goodnight to the owner. As she went out the door she took a deep breath trying to get the smell of smoke and stale beer from her head. The owner locked the door behind her and the sound sent a chill went up her spine. It was a moonless night and the dim lantern on the Inn was like an island in a black sea. Crossing the dark street, she walked past the silent brickworks; her footsteps were the only sound breaking the eerie quiet. She passed rows of finished brick piled high; they reminded her of gloomy chasms.

Suddenly an arm reached out of the shadows and pulled her into the darkness. Before she could scream a strong hand was clamped over her mouth and she was dragged deep into the inky catacombs. Finally he threw her roughly down on a pile of dirt. Terrified, Miriam fainted when she hit the ground. She awoke in the dark smelling his sour breath on her face and realizing he was on top of her. Sobbing, she pleaded for him to release her. He quietly growled "Shush now missy!" She recognized his voice -- the busboy from work! She tried to scream but before more than a gasp could escape her lips his big rough hands pressed into her neck cutting off her breath. He muttered angrily "I told ya to shush now!" She writhed in his grasp but he just pressed harder. Her lungs ached as she tried to breathe, she could feel consciousness slipping away as she scratched at his hands, horrible and rough. Her chest convulsed for the last time as her body went limp. A dark silence closed in and the last thing she could feel were his rough hands crushing her neck as her life ended. Miriam's final thought was holding her parents hands as she was being pulled away. Her fingers slipped past theirs, into darkness…

He shook her a bit then realized that he had strangled the life out of her. He had not meant to kill her but her neck was so delicate; her windpipe crushed under his grip. Frantically the busboy thought how to hide her body, and run away, far away. He dragged her deeper into the brickyard. Using his hands he buried her deep in a pile of sand where he hoped her body would be undiscovered for a while.

Miriam felt strange; she opened her eyes and watched as her limp body was covered with sand. She screamed in the busboys face "You, bastard, you murderer!" He showed no sign of hearing her as he finished his grisly task. She began to sob as it dawned that she was dead and no one could hear her anymore.

The busboy ran away and never returned; he was never called to account for his foul deed. When Miriam's body was discovered the authorities conducted a cursory investigation and forgot it as soon as they could. After all, Miriam was just a poor barmaid.

Frightened, lonely and sad, Miriam has waited as a ghost in the area of the old brickyard for over a hundred years. She could find no-one to tell her story to until Shelly. After telling it to us, Shelly helped Miriam cross over to her family and friends. She is at peace now and the scale by Shelly's desk is quiet.

The Boy with a Straw Hat

Late one dark and foggy night, Gail was driving home from a friend's house down West Henrietta Road. She passed the Baptist church on Erie Station Road. The fog was pretty thick and she was driving a bit slowly. In the distance on the right was a young boy. He was walking along wearing an old fashioned cotton shirt, jeans and a straw hat.

She thought it was very strange for a boy to be walking so late and slowed her car even more to look at him. He was barefoot as well; he looked like something out of a Norman Rockwell painting, she thought. The boy stopped and looked at her as she slowly passed by. She could see him looking a bit quizzically at her as she went by. Glancing to the left she saw the old carriage stop, where they used to make carriages and wagons in the 1800's. When she looked back towards the boy he was gone, the fog had swallowed all traces of him up.

West Henrietta Road was once known as the South Road. Even today if you follow it you would eventually end up in the Deep South. The original town of Henrietta was built on the South Road in 1818. As a major North South travel route there were of course many inns along the South Road. Many have been turned into private homes; others continue their tradition of hospitality like the Cartwright Inn. Of course there were numerous farms along this route as well as stops for the Underground Railroad. So seeing a ghost walking along the old South Road might not be that unusual.

Travel the South Road on a foggy night and you may catch a glimpse of the ghost boy as he walks along. Is he wondering what had become of the horses and carriages that used to travel the road? He will disappear into the fog as he nears the carriage stop, a place he liked to visit, to watch as they made carriages and wagons, the cars and trucks of his day…

31 - Ghosts of Old Rochesterville

The Wagon

It was a cold snowy day. Beth was driving home in her Ford Escort on route 259 by Parma Corners. The road took a dip and there was a culvert at the bottom to keep the road from flooding when it rained. She looked ahead and panicked – what seemed like a large moving van was at an angle blocking the road.

She began pumping her brakes, but the slick pavement was just making her car fishtail. Though slowing, there was no way she would stop in time. Bracing for impact, she held her breath. Her car slid closer; she realized the van was really a wagon, a wooden wagon. She could make out the canvas and wood planks. It was unreal as her car hit the wagon. Her car slowly passed right through it and stopped about 20 feet past it.

When Beth got out of her car to look, the wagon was gone. For a moment she could feel an intense pain and loss coming from the area. The feeling slowly faded. She drove home, trying to make sense of what she had seen and felt.

Slavery had been abolished in New York State. The Fugitive Slave Act (1850) did allow runaway slaves to be hunted, and recaptured with a bounty for each caught. This allowed what amounted to legal bounty hunters patrolling the routes taken by fleeing slaves. New York had many citizens who helped slaves to escape, despite fines and jail time, for anyone caught helping a runaway. This ghost story starts with two slave families running for freedom in a small town near Rochester called Parma. In Parma, the local Underground Railroad would sometimes use freight wagons to hide the runaways. They would bring them to Lake Ontario where the runaways would be put on boats headed for Canada, and freedom.

It was a cold rainy day in the mid 1800's. Two freight wagons pulled up to Parma Corners. They were loaded with dry goods for delivery. Two men in oilskin coats blocked the road. Their badges told the two men on the wagons that they were bounty hunters looking for runaway slaves. The horses snorted and stopped, the rain beat on the canvas tarps covering the wagons.

The owner of the wagons was in the lead; he was a well known local black businessman named Walter Vond. The second wagon was driven by another black man.

"Steady" said Vond to his wagon team. "What can I do for you?" he asked the two men.

"We are looking for several fugitive slaves we heard were in the area," the taller of the two said.

Vond replied "I own the dry goods store in town and this is my hired hand"

"We know who you are." The tall one said with disdain. The bounty hunters began to walk to the back of the second wagon.

The black man on the second wagon pulled his old hat a bit lower and quietly watched the two men. His heart raced as he hid his anxiety from the bounty hunters.

Vond looked back at the driver on the second wagon and said. "We have a big load here to deliver and I don't want to get it all wet while you are around looking. My customers won't like it." Ignoring him, one of the men went to the back gate of the wagon and lifted the canvas up.

His eyes opened wide as he saw three frightened faces looking at him. He was about to yell for his partner when the driver jumped off the wagon and tackled the man. The other bounty hunter ran to help, and the three men rolled in the mud exchanging blows.

Mr. Vond shouted "Come to this wagon!" and from under the other wagons tarp a woman and two children scampered out. They moved slowly at first, both scared and not wanting to leave their husband and father. The woman lifted the two children on Vond's wagon.

One of the bounty hunters seeing them got up and lunged at the three getting on the first wagon. The man managed to grab the woman's legs and dress just as she was climbing on the wagon. Vond lay on the whip, and the wagon tore away.

For a few seconds the woman desperately hung on to the wagon as it dragged both her and the bounty hunter behind it. Her strength was ebbing and despite her friend's hands trying to pull her in, she slipped, pulled away by the bounty hunter. They lay in the mud as Walter Vond's wagon pulled quickly away. They got up and the bounty man grabbed her arm.

Her husband had knocked the wind out of the other bounty man and climbed back on the wagon. He started it straight for the bounty hunter who was struggling with his wife. The bounty hunter leaped back and released the woman as the horses brushed him. Slowing slightly, the man reached down, grabbed his wife, and pulled her up into the wagon. He laid on the reigns, and the wagon sped up, turning on Hilton Parma Corners Road. The two bounty hunters raced to their horses and soon were in fast pursuit.

Vond's wagon was far ahead, lost in the heavy rain. The man and his wife were not so lucky; they looked back and saw the bounty hunters gaining on their wagon. He franticly urged on the horses faster. The wagon slid to and fro on the slippery muddy road. The road ahead was hard to see in the rain and mist; it dipped at the bottom of a hill and there was a flood washing out the road from the downpour.

Too late to stop, the horses slowed but the loaded wagon hit the water and jackknifed, throwing the man and woman into the water. They were swept away in the cold fast current. Battered from the fall and hit by debris washed in the freezing torrent she lost consciousness. As darkness overcame her, she thought of their children and knew that Walter had enough time to get them away to safety. Her husband was desperately trying to get to her but the heavy wet clothing and freezing water was dragging him under. To his last ounce of strength he reached out for her, and then his body, now lifeless, was carried by the current downstream.

When the two bounty hunters came to the wagon they jumped down from their mounts, and with sour expressions watched the man and wife's bodies wash down the gully in the flood. They had lost the first wagon, and knew it was going to take time to recover the bodies from this one.

If you are on route 259 near Parma in bad weather, slow down. You might just see a wagon blocking the road. If you do, say a prayer for that couple who died trying to live free.

Birdie Hart

If you happen to be walking or driving along Railroad Avenue or Orchard Street in Webster, NY on a dark night you may catch a glimpse of Birdie Hart walking along. Many have seen her walking that same route she and Erwin took on a fateful night in 1904.

In the land between Ridge Road and Lake Ontario, apples were grown as one of the major fruit crops. The town of

Webster, NY was known far and wide for its quality dried fruit. In the early 1900's, it was known as the dried apple Capitol of the world.

John W. Hallauer and Sons Evaporated Fruits was one of the 30 fruit companies that had its dry houses located on Railroad Avenue. They were the places where the apples were processed, dried and packaged for shipment by railroad.

The year was 1904, and the dry houses employed many locals; one, a single young woman by the name of Birdie Hart, worked at Hallauer & Sons.

Birdie had a boyfriend; his name was Erwin Smith. There was something about Smith that some folks found odd. Birdie and Erwin had been seeing each other for a while and though she knew he could be a bit strange at times he treated her well enough. Erwin loved her; while Birdie was fond of him, she did not share his feelings. His unrequited love frustrated him greatly. He tried to control his temper and not to show his building frustration but it did erupt into an occasional argument between them.

Erwin and Birdie went out one cool evening. The crescent moon peeked out from the clouds. Seeking some privacy, they went out behind the Hallauer dry house and talked as they walked along the large wooden building. The air was filled with the scent of late fall with the hint of dried apples. Erwin associated that sweet apple scent with Birdie. Tonight he would ask her to marry him; this was not the first time he had proposed, but he would press her for an answer.

As they walked along Erwin told her how much he loved her, then asked her for her answer about marrying him. Birdie had put him off before, but felt it was time to tell him that although she was fond of him, she knew he was not the man she wanted to marry.

With her refusal to marry Erwin's demeanor changed; he became more and more frustrated. He pleaded with her to marry him. Finally Birdie blurted out: "Erwin, I don't love you."

In that instant, his frustration became hurt and then blind anger. "You, you, don't love me?" he stammered and with that he raised a hand and struck Birdie on the side of her head. She fell back striking her head on a rock; horror and panic quickly replaced his rage as he realized just what he had done.

She was limp and he was sure he had killed her. His stomach knotted and he kneeled down and looked at poor Birdie lying unmoving on the grass. He shuddered, frightened at the thought of what he had done, then he softly cried "Why, why did she reject me?" At his core Erwin was a coward and rather than face up to his wretched deed he desperately tried to figure what to do next. "The dry house," he thought "hide her body in the dry house!"

Yes, he could make it appear like an accident in there. Looking around to be sure no one had seen what had happened he forced the side door open and carried her inside.

He placed her body into a corner near the basket rack. The dry house was filled with sweet scent of drying apples. The scent that once reminded him of Birdie - now burned his senses with her rejection of him. Frantically he pulled the wooden baskets from the rack and piled them over her along with old newspaper that had been used to line the racks. Desperate to be rid of her and that scent of apples, he struck a match and set the paper and baskets on fire in several places. As he stood looking at Birdie's funeral pyre, mesmerized by the flames that were quickly spreading, he heard a faint moan from under the burning pile. Thinking he must be mad for she could not be still alive he covered his ears and ran from the building as the crackling roar of the fire drowned out her pitiful cries. Erwin disappeared into the night to make his escape.

Under the rapidly burning pile smoke built up, and heat began to reach her. Birdie's last confused thought was "No

Erwin, I don't love you. My head why does it hurt, it's so hot..."
The smoke mercifully overcame Birdie before the flames reached
her.

The fire was visible through the open door and windows.
Nearby neighbors saw the flames, gave the alarm and helped
form a bucket brigade until the local Fire Company could get
there. Soon they had the blaze under control and saved the
building. As they cleaned out the burnt debris they found poor
Birdie's scorched body under the pile of ashes and a few charred
bits and pieces of baskets. Her death and the fire were ruled
murder and arson.

In the end Erwin Smith was caught and convicted for his
foul deed. It was not reported what punishment was sentenced.
And poor Birdie was laid to rest, yet she is still restless. She
wanders the streets near the old dry house, still looking for Erwin
to tell him she won't marry him, touching her face where he hit
her and wondering why it was so hot on such a cool night.

43 - Ghosts of Old Rochesterville

Great Balls of Fire!

The Distillery sits across from Mount Hope Cemetery. It's a great place to grab some wings and a beer with friends. The Distillery itself is an interesting place; some of the staff thinks there may be a ghost there that plays tricks on them from time to time. In the basement is an area that may have been part of a old tunnel system, now blocked off. Several Houses in the area had tunnels, used for the Underground Rail Road and smuggling bootlegged liquor.

One of the night managers went on one of my ghost walks. After the walk we sat down at the Distillery and she told me about her encounter with a strange apparition late one night.

It was closing time and she, as the night manager, let the staff out and locked the door of the Distillery. They were heading for their cars when one of the staff said "Look at that!" She pointed to the cemetery across the street.

Everyone looked toward the cemetery and saw what the manager described as a "fiery glowing ball" in the distance. For a while all stood there staring at the glowing orb until they realized it was getting larger. Slowly it seemed like it was getting closer to the cemetery gate, directly across from them.

Totally silent, it was growing larger and larger. They could see it was glowing red and yellow with flames enveloping it.

As if the thought struck all of them at once they said "Let's get out of here!" They ran to their cars and quickly drove off not waiting to see if the ball of flames would get any closer.

The manager stopped by the cemetery the next day. She searched the area where they had seen it but nothing was scorched, no sign at all that a huge burning orb was ever there.

Are You Warm Yet?

I do ghost walks in and around Rochester. On one of them we go along the fence of Mount Hope Cemetery. Mount Hope is a majestic Victorian Cemetery full of beautiful memorials, obelisks, sarcophagi, mausoleums, crypts, headstones and more all set in a most bizarre landscape of hills, sinkholes and winding roads.

One cold October night on a ghost walk, Donna, one of the guests, told me she was getting warm on her left side. As we walked on she was getting warmer and warmer. We were unable to figure out why she was so warm. By the end of our walk Donna was getting very hot on her left side

We chatted for a while after the ghost walk ended. She told me that she was empathic, a person who can literally feel another's emotion or pain. This is not limited to the living souls around her, for she can also feel the pain and anguish felt by the departed.

As an example of her empathic ability, Donna then told me of a trip she and her friend had taken to Gettysburg. She was walking on Baltimore Street, by the house in which Jennie Wade was killed. Jennie Wade has the sad distinction of being the only civilian killed in Gettysburg during the battle. The house, now a museum, is reputed to be haunted by Jennie's ghost.

On that fateful morning, July 12 in 1863, Jennie was kneading bread dough in the kitchen; she and her mother were baking bread to give to Union soldiers.

In those days it was common practice for sharpshooters to check their aim by shooting at the doorknob on the front door. At 8:30 AM, one Confederate marksman took aim at the doorknob on the house. Inside, Jennie was unaware of her appointment with destiny. Concentrating on the brass doorknob, he slowly pulled the trigger until the gun roared and discharged a cloud of smoke. Looking at the door, he saw that he had missed his mark but hit the door. The bullet had indeed ripped through that door, then through the kitchen door and, alas, struck poor Jennie in her back shoulder and went through her body. It was a mortal wound and she fell, dying within moments.

As Donna walked by the door which had been hit by the Confederate sharp shooter, she fell to her knees with a sharp pain from her back to her throat. Her hands went to her throat as she began to choke, unable to breathe. Her friend helped her up and half dragged her away from the house. She soon recovered; the only explanation was that Jennie's ghost had allowed her to literally feel the moment when Jennie was shot.

After she told me the story of Gettysburg, I asked if her left side was still feeling warm. She said "It was." I smiled and said, "You know, the walk takes us closer to the crematorium; it's just down there to your left."

The Dark Shadow

of Lizzie Borden

While not a Rochester story this happened to a woman from Rochester who was on vacation. Two friends, Dee and Sue were vacationing near Fall River, Massachusetts. Both had an interest in ghosts and the macabre, so they decided to visit the site of the Lizzie Borden murders.

The story of course is infamous; on August 4, 1892, Mr. and Mrs. Borden (it should be noted that Mrs. Borden was Lizzie's stepmother) were murdered in their home in Fall River,

Massachusetts. It was gruesome, violent and bloody. Both had been struck repeatedly by an ax or hatchet in their heads.

Their daughter Lizzie was considered unstable; consequently she was arrested and tried for the crime but acquitted by the jury. The crime and trial spawned this popular rhyme:

Lizzie Borden took an axe

And gave her mother forty whacks,

When she saw what she had done,

She gave her father forty-one.

Lizzie remained single and lived the remainder of her life in Falls River; she was always looked at with suspicion by people. The house is currently a museum and Bed & Breakfast.

The girls arrived late in the day just as the museum was closing. They talked with the curator for a few minutes and he suggested they visit the local cemetery where Lizzie Borden is buried.

They were game for an adventure and went to visit the Oak Grove Cemetery. The monument was easy to find. Lizzie is buried a few feet from the family memorial; her grave is marked by a simple stone with her name inscribed upon it. The sun was setting as they stood at the grave. Just then a strange unsettling chill came over Dee. It was overwhelming her so much that she insisted they leave immediately.

As they drove further away from the cemetery the feeling lessened. They went to a restaurant but the uneasiness was still there through dinner and continued as she got into bed at the motel. Her friend, Sue, was fast asleep in the next bed but Dee tossed and turned.

Thoughts of the cemetery flashed through her mind. They were cold and foreboding. In her mind she watched as darkness devoured Lizzie's grave stone. The coldness of the thoughts seeped into her body; she could not get warm despite the thick comforter.

Glancing at the clock, she saw it was midnight when she looked up and noticed a movement on the ceiling. It was very dark in the room but the shadowy shape was darker, pitch black. It moved like a crab along the ceiling. A chill went down her spine and her breath came in short gasps as she watched the black shadow crawl to a spot directly above her. Suddenly the shadow dropped from the ceiling down on top of her. She covered her face with her right arm, closed her eyes and screamed into the falling darkness.

The next thing she remembered was a glow of warmth; taking a deep breath she opened her eyes. The sun shone through the curtains. It was a beautiful morning. When Sue woke up, Dee asked her if she had heard anything during the night, and she said "No." The strange cold feelings were gone as well as the shadow creature, chased away by the warm sunshine. It never appeared again to Dee; perhaps it went back to the cemetery where it dwelled and lays waiting for another to haunt...

More Shadow People

Shadow people - shadows that look human in outline but there is no one around who could be casting them. They can be seen even in the dark as being blacker than the night. Here are two encounters I have had with shadow people.

One early evening in August of 2005 I took a walk with a few friends in Mt. Hope Cemetery. One of the members of the group was an older gentleman who was quite gifted as a psychic.

As we passed one of the oldest sections of graves, dating back to the 1700's on a ridge about 100 yards distant was a shadow watching us. This shadow was not attached to a person and it disappeared a moment after I saw him; I got the distinct impression it was male. The older gentleman saw me looking at the Ridge, smiled and said "It seems they are watching us."

At Rolling Hills Mall in East Betheny, NY, there are regular ghost hunts. The current owners bought it as a mini-mall but it has had many uses. It was originally built in 1827 to be the Genesee County poor house; a few of its other uses include an insane asylum, orphanage, and nursing home. One can hardly imagine the suffering and death that happened through the years. Consequently many former residents have you might say, stayed around.

On one of the ghost hunts at Rolling Hills I was in one of the dark hallways. The lights were off in most of the building except the exits, cafeteria, and the gift shop.

I was looking in an infrared camcorder, and a group of ghost hunters had just passed me in the hall. I then saw, walking about 15 feet behind them, a dark shadow. I watched this shadow follow the group as it walked down the hall. It was then I realized the camcorder was in standby and not recording.

57 - Ghosts of Old Rochesterville

Sick Children

This story comes from Fairport, NY. Originally part of Perinton, Fairport was born when the Erie Canal came through in the early 1820's. It became a busy canal port with the shipping of local agricultural crops and several industries including Cobb Preserving and Deland Chemical.

On Whitney Road in Fairport stands an older house, built in the 1800's. Back then the land that Fairport is now on was swampy. Before the canal helped to drain the swamps there were many insect bourn illnesses, usually they were generically called "swamp fever." Back then, "swamp fever" carried a much higher mortality rate than in the present day, especially when it struck children.

Today the house is owned by a couple who raised two lovely daughters there. Now grown, the older daughter Teresa told me a story from her childhood.

As a young girl, Teresa was occasionally visited by a small dark figure. No one else in the house ever saw it. Her mom just said it was her imagination.

Teresa felt it was not going to hurt her; sometimes she would even say hello to it. The shadow would just watch her for a bit then disappear.

One night she woke up to see it sitting on her bed. It seemed to be looking at her, and then disappeared. Soon Teresa began to feel cold, and ill with a stomach ache. Burying herself under her blankets she shivered, feeling cold and sick the rest of the night until daybreak, when the mysterious symptoms vanished.

Later that the morning, she went into her younger sister's room. As soon as Teresa entered, her sister told of the same small dark figure who had sat on her bed in the night. The younger sister said she felt sick to her stomach for a while after the shadow's visit. Teresa then told her of the shadows visit to her room.

The shadow ghost was never again seen by either of them. The sisters had no desire to see it again after that uncomfortable night. Teresa always believed it was the ghost of a child who had died in the house from some childhood illness.

The Ouija Board

of Captain Kidd

The Ouija or "talking board" is supposed to divine answerers from the "spirits." Those seated around the board would lightly touch the planchette and it would move around, spelling out the answer. There are a number of beautiful boards, some hand crafted and others mass produced, many have become collector's items. Who invented the Ouija board is unknown, though the first patent for the modern style Ouija board was awarded in 1891 to Charles Kennard.

The Ouija board has acquired a dangerous and even evil reputation for attracting bad entities. Even today, some people will not even enter a room that has a Ouija board in it. Many people have had strange experiences when using the Ouija Board. This is a story about a young girl named Ann and her friends first and last encounter with a Ouija board.

When Ann was young, she was fascinated with pirates, so begins the story of the Ouija board of Captain Kidd. Back then, there were no video games, children loved to play using imagination. Ann's favorite game was playing pirate. The neighborhood became the high seas where they sailed from one adventure to another, swords swinging, peg legs clacking on the deck, eye patches -- and -- "Aaargh" the most important thing, the search for pirate's treasure!

Ann fondly recalled those days when she was a young girl, she and her friends would play pirate every chance they could. Each day they sailed far and wide in their backyards looking for buried treasure. If they only had a real pirate treasure map marked with an X; apparently the ones they made from notebook paper and crayons were not as accurate in marking where those gold doubloons lay buried as they had hoped.

Now where to find a real treasure map? They had searched and found no pirates, living or otherwise in the neighborhood. Likewise they had dug a lot of holes looking for treasure; no maps had they found in any of them. Even the library where there were so many stories of pirates and their treasure – none had ever mentioned New York State, and certainly not Rochester as the preferred spot to bury treasure!

One day Ann and her friends found an old Ouija Board in a heap of discarded items by the curb. A real Ouija Board to talk to spirits – their minds raced with thoughts of the ways they could use it! They could forget the crayon maps and contact a real pirate, and ask him where he had buried his treasure. Surely some pirate must have visited upstate NY to find a good spot to bury his gold doubloons. Now to decide just which pirate to ask? Well, they figured there's really only one to ask, the most famous, most nefarious pirate there ever was, Captain Kidd. He had loads of treasure, and according to the stories, he buried it up and down the East Coast! Why, there were stories of treasure hunters still looking for his treasure chests that have never been found.

Deciding that they needed a dark place to use the Ouija Board, the children took their prize and went into Ann's bedroom closet. It was large enough for all four of them to fit, once they moved some shoes and a box of stuff to make room. Closing the door, it was nice and dark. They sat down in a circle, struck a match and lit the candle; its flame lit the closet in an eerie orange glow, while the burnt match lent a sulfurous smell to the darkness.

In the flickering light, they placed the board in the middle of the circle and invoked the board to speak with the ghost of Captain Kidd, the pirate. Next, they placed their finger tips on the planchette. As soon they did, it felt a bit colder in the closet, and a shiver went up Ann's spine.

Under their fingers, the planchette strained to move and spell out something. Frightened and shaking, they let go of the planchette. At that moment, the closet became ice cold. Ann was sitting with her back against the wall, and began to get up. Behind Ann, from out of the wall formed two large hands that grabbed her shoulders; big, strong, icy fingers pressed into her. She screamed as they roughly pushed her back down, holding her there. The other children began screaming, pushed the closet door open, and ran downstairs. The hands let go, and Ann dashed out after the others. As she ran, Ann could have sworn she heard a deep laugh that resonated from the closet. They didn't stop until they were out of the house, still shaking and screaming.

When the children had gathered enough courage to go back upstairs to Ann's room, the Ouija Board, planchette, and candle were there as they had left them. They carefully returned the Ouija Board to the same pile of junk by the curb. After narrowly escaping the captain's grasp, they never touched another Ouija Board again. It would seem that even in death, Captain Kidd does not want to share his treasure.

The Gray Lady

of Fishell Road

On Fishell Road, near Route 15, is a small forgotten graveyard, with about fifteen graves. It sits on the south shore of Honeoye Creek. Only three of the headstones remain, and they are knocked down, and nearly hidden in the grass.

The summer of 2006, Sandy moved into the house across the road from the small graveyard. She liked to walk her dog, an energetic cocker spaniel named Sunny, every day along the road. One day Sunny managed to get free and ran off. He headed right for the graves and was circling the headstones when Sandy caught up with him. As she put the leash on him she noticed the name on one of the gravestones; it was Catherine. Thinking no more about it, Sandy walked the dog home.

That evening as she lay in bed, Sandy glanced at the mirror door on the closet. Her heart skipped a beat as she watched a gray shadow silently pacing back and forth. A slight heaviness could be felt in the air as the shadow paced. The shadow was of a slender woman in a full dress. Then the gray shadow walked past the closet and vanished. Just as the shadow vanished, the name Catherine flashed into Sandy's mind. She wondered if something had followed her home from the old graveyard the dog had run to that afternoon. The gray shadow came back to visit Sandy's room several times in the next two weeks.

Then, in the late evenings, the living room stereo began to turn on. No one was downstairs; the dog was in her room, sleeping. Most recently, Sandy's office paper shredder turned itself on in the night; she had to unplug it to get it to turn off.

While not a regular visitor, Catherine stops by from time to time, sometimes playing with the stereo and occasionally visiting the bedroom. One recent evening, Sandy was sitting in the living room when several CD cases popped out of the CD rack onto the floor. It would seem Catherine has a curiosity about today's music?

71 - Ghosts of Old Rochesterville

Ghost of Emily Post

Carol bought her house about 6 years ago and has learned to coexist with a prim and proper spirit. Her home is in Greece, a suburb of Rochester. Originally farmland, Greece is now a popular suburb to live in for many of the folks who work at Kodak and other local industries.

When she first moved in, nothing out of the ordinary happened in the house. She settling in quickly and really loved the new place. After a few months some strange things began to happen. At first the lights and TV would turn on in the middle of the night.

Carol suspected she might not be alone in the house. She thought a ghost who playing with the lights was amusing. But something even more bizarre began happening shortly after, in the silverware drawer.

Set in her ways, Carol liked to place the knives, then forks then spoons in the silverware drawer from right to left. About a month after the lights and TV began turning on, she was surprised to find her silverware drawer rearranged. She placed the silverware back as she had it before, but the next morning it was neatly rearranged again. It seemed Carol's way to organize the silverware was not acceptable to the ghost.

Not deterred, Carol arranges her silverware every day, and every morning the silverware is rearranged. The forks first, then the knives, and lastly spoons, just as Emily post would have set a table. Apparently Carol's home has a ghost with a sense of etiquette.

May I Have a Ride?

This ghost story is a classic; you can find many similar ones from all parts of the country. It is known as a "vanishing hitchhiker" story, the woman who told it to me swears it happened.

The events in this story took place several years ago to a young woman named Debbie who lives in the small town of

Basom, West of Rochester. It was a Wednesday, and, like most Wednesdays Debbie was shopping at the Tops grocery store in Batavia, NY. From out of nowhere an older woman walked up to her and asked, "My name is Kate and I hate to bother you but could please give me a ride?" The woman seemed very nice. Kate began to explain that she had just come in on the bus, her daughter was not here to pick her up and she had no way to get there.

The first thought that struck the Debbie was, of all the other people in the store, why ask her? Then it struck her, why had the woman come all the way to Tops for a ride when the bus stop was in another part of town. She remembered it used to be just across the street about two years earlier before the bus company had moved it across town.

Debbie felt sorry for the woman and agreed to drive her. When asked where her daughter lived, Kate replied "Lewiston Road in Oakfield." a nearby town. Surprised, Debbie replied that she knew where the road was because she used to live there as a child. As they drove along the women reminisced about the area. They turned onto the road and soon Kate pointed to her daughter's house. "No!" Debbie exclaimed; her heart skipped a beat "That's the house I used to live in."

Upon hearing that, Kate smiled and insisted that she must come in for a visit. They pulled in the driveway and Kate went into the house, Debbie followed.

When Debbie walked into the room the older woman was nowhere to be seen. On the floor was a young child, he was perhaps two years old, smiling and laughing. She wondered where the older woman went; a moment later a woman's voice came out of another room "you are always so happy on Wednesdays." The child's mother came out of another room looked at her strangely, said "Who are you and are you doing in my house?"

A bit mystified, Debbie told her who she was and explained that she gave an older woman a ride here from the Batavia Tops because no one was there to pick her up. And how surprised Debbie was because she used to live here as a child. Puzzled, the mom said that there was no one else here. Debbie described the lady and walked to a photograph hanging on the wall and said "This is her; she said her name was Kate."

The young mother's hands went up to her mouth and her face went pale. "That's my mother. She used to take the bus from Buffalo almost every Wednesday to visit here and I would pick her up at the old bus stop across from the Tops grocery store in Batavia. She passed away two years ago, about the time they moved the old bus stop."

The two women stared at each other not knowing what to say. The child ignored them and was chatting happily away as he did every Wednesday when grandma stopped by to visit.

The Friendly Ghost

As a child Tammy would visit her cousin Lisa, in Wyoming County. Her cousin had an imaginary friend she called Copley. She would talk to her friend every day. When Tammy would sleep over she would wake up to find a chair drawn up to her cousin's side of the bed. Lisa would be talking quietly with Copley.

Her parents thought it amusing that their daughter had an imaginary friend. There were plenty of children nearby and Lisa enjoyed playing with them, so her parents were not worried.

On the property next to theirs was an abandoned house. The owner had died many years before Lisa's family had moved next door. The neighborhood children all said it was haunted. Lisa paid no heed to the tales and often played by the fence of the abandoned property.

One day an older woman who lived down the road saw the girl by the fence talking to her imaginary friend when she stopped by for a visit. "I am curious about who your girl could be talking to." She asked Lisa's mom as they sat at the kitchen table. Mom replied "Lisa has an imaginary friend she liked to talk to." Both women laughed.

Lisa came in from playing and said hello. The old woman smiled and said "I understand you have a friend you like to talk to." Lisa smiled back and replied "Yes, he is the nicest man; his name is Copley." Hearing that name the woman's face turned pale. She said "Oh my. Copley was the name of the man who used to own the house where your daughter was just playing. He died years ago before you moved here. He was a sweet, friendly gentleman who loved children."

Lisa smiled and whispered "yes he is."

The Flag

One early evening in August, 2005 a few of my friends decided to ghost hunt in Mount Hope Cemetery in Rochester, NY. This was the same trip we saw the shadow ghost (More Shadow People). There were five of us, including Ray a gifted psychic. We rendezvous at the old crematorium, a stone building with a very tall chimney that hinted at its true use.

It was warm, humid and there was no breeze. The cottonwood trees were releasing their seeds and the waning sun backlit thousands of cottony balls gently floating down in the still air.

Mount Hope is a wonderful old cemetery with unique natural features. We walked the winding roads untill we came to a section with several older graves about sixty feet ahead of us. One had a small American flag next to the headstone. For some reason I stopped and looked at the grave for a few seconds.

As I watched the flag it began to flutter. The rest of the group stopped and watched. The flag was moving as if a light breeze was blowing on it. Not a bit of a breeze was evident, the grass and leaves were dead still, yet the flag was moving.

Slowly we walked closer to the flag. It continued to move in the nonexistent breeze. As we approached to about twenty five feet the flag straightened out as if in a strong wind for a second then fell back unmoving.

I looked at Ray who was staring intently at the flag and asked him what his impression was. "There's a little girl lying on the grave, she was playing with the flag. She came to visit her father." He said.

We stayed for a couple of minutes taking photographs and trying to get EVP's (electronic voice phenomenon) then moved on. The flag remained still, Ray said the girl was tired and was lying down next to her dad.

Checkers Anyone?

Last summer a young mother was rummaging through antiques at one of the many shops on Park Avenue in Rochester. She found a nice old wooden checker board set. She bought it, thinking it would make a great decoration for their son's room. As soon as she got home she put it up on his room's wall.

In the middle of the night, several days later, their son crawled into their bed saying a girl was staring at him. Mom hustled him back to bed and assured him it was a dream. As she sat there with him, the lights flickered on and off. An eerie feeling crept over her, but she shook it off as silly.

A few nights later her son cried out and mom ran to his room. She stopped at the door and saw a little girl in a yellow dress and white bonnet standing at the foot of his bed; the girl turned to look at her then vanished. This began to happen on a regular basis until it hit mom that the ghostly girl started to show up after she bought the checker board.

She took the checker board out of her son's room and put it in the play room. From then on the little girl stopped looking in on their son and seems content to reside in the play room where the lights occasionally flicker and if you peek in late at night you might see her in her white bonnet and yellow dress. The family sort of likes having a ghost in the house, as long as it doesn't interfere with a good nights sleep.

Man with the Mustache

On Bay Road in Webster sits an old farmhouse; it was built in 1834. In the 1990's, Jackie was a young girl living there with her family.

She would occasionally see a man with a handlebar moustache watching her in the upstairs hallway. He would just stand quietly at the end of the hall, watching her as she walked to her room.

Jackie had told her parents but they had never seen him. After a while she got used to seeing him in the hall and just accepted him as part of the old house.

Several years ago, her parents began remodeling the kitchen. They tore the floor up, and, as in many old homes, there was a layer of old newspapers under the old linoleum. In with the old papers was an old photograph, a man with a handlebar moustache.

Jackie's mom showed the picture to her saying, "We found this photograph under the old flooring. Do you recall the man you always saw upstairs? The moustache reminded me." Jackie looked at it and said "Oh my God! That's the man who used to watch me in the hall."

Montezuma's Revenge

This story came to me by one of my fellow ghost hunting meet up members. They say ghosts and other entities can attach themselves to objects. If you bring the haunted item home you will bring the attached spirit also.

Sharon and her fiancé Todd, received a clay sun god ornament from a friend who was visiting Mexico. It was a strange looking clay sculpture with clay feathers and a very Aztec nose. Todd liked it very much and hung it on his apartment's living room wall.

When he was home he noticed the lights would occasionally flicker on and off. He thought little of it as bigger things were on his mind. He was going to marry Sharon soon and build a house in Webster, NY, on Gravel Road.

Sharon and Todd got married and built their house. The things in his old apartment were packed in boxes and shipped to the new house. It was several months before the boxes were unpacked. The sun god was put on the new family room wall.

Within days of the idol hanging on the wall, Todd started feeling ill. Nothing really serious or life threatening, just feeling drained, with headaches one after the other and no let up. Other things began happening as well, strange things.

The lights in the family room flickered while they sat and watched TV. Doors that they had left closed were wide open when they went back into the room, open doors would slam shut.

To add to this both Sharon and Todd began to feel that they were being watched, especially in the family room.

Then one day while Sharon was vacuuming she looked to the kitchen doorway, standing there was a hazy dark shadow with broad shoulders silently watching her. Startled, she dropped the vacuum hose and it vanished. When Todd returned home from work that day she told him about the shadow that was watching her. His face paled a bit and he said "I didn't want to scare you but I saw a shadow figure too, in the basement a couple of weeks ago."

They decided that they would ask a friend who was a pastor to come in and bless the house. It was a stressful time waiting for the pastor to arrive. Every so often one of them would catch the shadow out of the corner of their eye, watching them.

When the pastor arrived he started in the attic of the house. He carefully looked in each room, saying prayers and shutting the door when he was finished. When he got to the family room he was immediately drawn to the sun god. He told the couple that the sculpture was the source of the problems and he asked permission to break it.

Without hesitation they said "Yes."

They brought him a hammer. He laid the sculpture on the coffee table and wrapped it in a thick cloth so no pieces would escape. Raising the hammer he whispered a prayer. He struck the idol, it screamed as it shattered. They heard footsteps then the outside door slammed shut. They were all a bit shaken. The atmosphere in the house felt different, as if a weight had been lifted from them.

"Is it gone?" the wife asked. The pastor nodded and took the sun gods shattered remains and told them he would dispose of it.

The pastor tied the cloth up then put the wrapped pieces on the passenger seat of his car and drove away. He had not driven far when he began to feel queasy. Soon he felt very warm and his throat began to close – as if unseen hands were slowly choking him. Glancing at the remains he was shocked to see the dark shadow next to him. It was staring at him, its eyes glowed a dark angry red.

The car too seemed to be fighting him, it became more difficult to steer. The car weaved back and forth, the pastor fought with all his strength to control it as he gasped for air. He was able to slow down and pull the car into a plaza on Ridge Road. Stopping by a dumpster he grabbed the cloth containing the idol and struggled out of the car, he threw the bundle of pieces into the dumpster.

As soon as he threw it the invisible hands let go of his throat. Falling to his knees the pastor took deep breaths and rubbed his neck, while saying a silent prayer of thanks. Soon the evil thing would be buried in a landfill he thought, and prayed it would bother no one else again.

Back at the house, Todd was already feeling better. In a couple of days the mysterious symptoms that had been plaguing him were completely gone.

The house is now quiet. Sharon - she is now interested in ghost hunting. And Todd, well he learned a new meaning of "Montezuma's Revenge."

91 - Ghosts of Old Rochesterville

The Manitou

Manitou Beach is named after the Manitou, the Indian spirits who watch and protect the land. Legend has it that interesting things can be seen around Manitou Beach late at night. This appealed to a group of four young college friends, two girls and two guys, who had heard about the legend. One weekend they decided to go in search of the Manitou.

They went to Captain Braddock's, a restaurant (now closed) on the bay. The restaurant owner was a friend who allowed them to stay after hours and use the place as their observation base – it had large windows that looked out on the bay. It seemed like a perfect spot to look out on the bay area for any Manitou passing by.

The owner told them to have fun and feel free to have some snacks he had left in the fridge for them. Things were quiet as they looked out the windows for any signs of the Manitou. As they kept their vigil, they talked about the Manitou and other ghostly legends, an eerie feeling began to settle over them.

About midnight one of the guys went into the kitchen to get the tray of snacks. Moments later they heard him scream. Rushing to the kitchen they saw the young man paralyzed with fear looking out the window over the sink. Something was banging aggressively against the glass, and then stopped suddenly. All at once it was unnaturally quiet as they rushed to the window to see what was out there.

Whatever he had seen was gone save for distinct scratches on the glass and window frame. The young man was cold, pale and breathing heavily as they helped him to the front room and sat him down.

One of the girls gave him a glass of water and he mumbled: "I'm ok, ok." He began to tell them what had happened. He had gone to wash his hands when in the window was a huge dark thing. "It just stood there covered in long stringy hair; looking at me with glowing red eyes. I must have screamed then," he said. "It snarled, God it had long fangs, then it slashed its clawed hand across the window. Then the thing banged on the window and that's when you guys came in."

By then the group was not worried about finding the Manitou; it seemed to have found them; they were worried about surviving the night. They were too frightened to go outside and get in their car so they decided to stay at the restaurant until daylight. They each picked up something with which to defend themselves with should that thing get in. Huddled together they spent a restless night jumping at every sound till the sun's golden glow cast the feeling of evil away.

They went around the building to take a look at the window. There were no footprints and the scratch marks on the glass had faded away, but the marks in the wood were still there. Four claws from the Manitou's hand.

Man in Black

Mary's boyfriend lived in Hilton, a small town west of Rochester. Although Hilton is known for apple orchards and small town living, but perhaps there are darker things dwelling there.

Every time Mary was in his house, several areas would feel cold and despondent, most strongly the master bedroom and stairway. While the feelings bothered her, she did her best to ignore them. The feelings had nothing to do with her boyfriend Todd; they seemed to be attached to the house.

Suppressing the feelings worked for a while, until she began to be aware of something watching her. The eerie sensations were worst in the stairway. Then one evening she was over for a visit, and there by the stairs was a man, dressed in black, and leaning against the wall. His arms were crossed and he was scowling at her. The way he looked at Mary sent shivers down her spine. She called Todd in, and pointed at the dark specter, but he saw nothing.

Then, faintly, she could hear a woman crying from up the stairs. Mary followed the sobbing to the master bedroom. In the room she saw the ghost of a young woman lying on the bed; she was crying. When Mary walked closer, the ghost looked at her, and pleaded for Mary's help to escape. The sobbing ghost told her that the man in black keeps her locked away in the bedroom, abusing her for his carnal desires.

It had begun so long ago in the early 1800's. He was a wealthy landowner who had had just settled in Hilton. He met her on a business trip to New England and was smitten by her beauty. He had convinced her to come for a visit to see his new property.

At first he seemed quite nice but soon he showed his true nature. He was an avaricious, controlling, and heartless man. His real personality repulsed and even frightened her. She told him that she was not interested and would be going back to New England immediately.

At that his eyes filled with rage, and said "You will not be leaving, my dear."

He roughly led her to the upstairs bedroom and locked her in. He treated her as a slave, for his dark soul desired only submission to his will.

She was a prisoner in his home; weeks dragged into months. She tried to resist submitting to his carnal desires, but he forced himself violently upon her. Desperate and despondent, she could not go on.

One evening she sat on the bed holding a pair of sewing scissors in her hands. For a long while she stared at them. Hearing a noise -- his footsteps on the stairs -- she raised the scissors to her breast. He opened the door and as she looked at the face she hated so, she smiled and fell to the floor face down. The scissors were driven deep in her breast. He rushed to her and clutched her head in his hands and looked deep into her dying eyes.

Blood trickled from her mouth as she softly said "I am free..."

As the cold darkness closed around her, the last words she heard was his angry curse -- "Death will not free you from me!"

Mary felt sorry for the ghostly lady. She continued to see Todd for a while; though she began to avoid going over to his house because the ghost of the man in black made her too uncomfortable.

As for the poor despondent ghost lady, in life the man in black possessed her body; in death he possessed her soul. So if you should be in a house in Hilton and see the ghostly figure of a man in black, listen carefully for you may hear the sound of a crying woman coming from upstairs.

Dreaming of Daddy

Ann Marie's dad had passed away about a year ago. It had been a difficult year for Ann Marie, her sister, and their mother. Just a week ago her sister had moved away. No one had gone in to clean her room yet. There were a few things to put away and clean up.

That night Ann Marie had a dream. Her father stood by her bed, smiling. He took her hand and led her into her sister's room. He asked her to look under the bed. She did, and found a garbage bag. Her father said "Open it." She reached for the bag, and pulled it out. Untwisting the tie, she began to open the bag. Suddenly the alarm buzzed and Ann Marie woke up.

The dream was still fresh in her memory, and Dad had felt so real. She jumped out of bed and ran down the hall to her sister's room. Opening the door, the room was just like she had seen it in the dream. She bent over and looked under the bed. Her heart raced, for there was the garbage bag she had seen in her dream.

Fingers trembling she opened it up, and there, on top of the crumpled paper and other junk, was a letter. She pulled it out and read it.

Tears welled in her eyes as she read; it was a very touching letter and poem that her sister had written to their father. Ann Marie called her sister and told her what happened. Her sister said that she had written it, but she misplaced it, and had forgotten about it. Ann Marie was glad her father hadn't forgotten where it was…

Family Ghosts

Many families have a ghost story or two; it is always interesting when getting together at family gatherings to hear some of the stories. Here are two stories from my family. Both are about my father, the first when he was a child, and the second after he passed away.

The Coal Bin

One story my father, Ray, used to tell happened when he was a child in Catskill, NY. He and a group of friends went exploring. They had found their way into the cellar of an old house near Bridge Street, through an open window. They were exploring the dark and creepy cellar. As Ray walked past the wooden coal bin, a black hand reached out and grabbed him by the neck. He struggled and cried "Let me go!"

The rest of the kids screamed and scrambled to get out of the window, leaving him struggling to get away from the hand. It lifted him off the ground and was pulling him inside the dark bin. At that moment he heard a hiss, and a stray cat leaped from a nearby shelf onto the hand. The cat dug in with its claws, the hand released him, and Ray rushed out the window.

The next day the children's curiosities led them back to that basement. Armed with sticks, just in case the hand and its owner were still there, they went back through the window. The coal bin was empty except for a bit of coal. Next to the bin was the lifeless body of a cat, the same one that had saved my father's life.

A Familiar Visitor

My grandmother, his mom, lived to be 103. She had quite a life, outlived three of her children including, my dad. I would go to visit her in Catskill several times a year, after my dad had passed away. Now at her age, grandma's mind was forgetful, but she still recalled most of the family. Whenever she saw me, she would smile and tell me that my dad stops by to visit her now and then.

I always wondered about that until my Aunt Fran told me this story. Aunt Fran now sleeps in the same room my dad had when he was a child. She told me that occasionally she wakes up and the sheets on the end of her bed are pressed down as if a child had been sitting on the bed.

She told me she can feel my father's presence at times. I like to think he is visiting the people and places that were dear to him in life.

Grandparent Stories

The Proper Order of Things

Jill loved her grandparents. They were very old fashioned. In their living room were individual portraits, grandpa's hung above grandma's.

When Jill was a child she had taken them down to look at them, then put them back up. When she did, she put grandma on the higher hook. Grandpa walked in and laughed, then told her that his picture belonged above grandma's. Jill asked him, "Why, Grandpa?" He replied, "That is the proper order of things." He gave her a hug and a kiss, and she ran off to play.

After they passed away, she inherited the pictures of grandma and grandpa that had hung in their living room. Jill put them on her living room wall. At first she hung them level next to each other. Every morning she would find grandpa's picture on the floor.

Jill re-hung the photographs, this time putting grandma above grandpa. Just as before, in the morning she found the picture of grandpa on the floor. After a couple of days she had a thought, and placed grandpa's portrait above grandma's. The next morning both pictures were still on the wall.

Now Jill has moved 3 times, and every time she hung her grandparents' pictures in the new home she would first hang grandma's picture over grandpa's just to see what would happen. Sure enough, every time she did, grandpa's portrait was on the floor the next morning.

She found that when grandpa's picture was above grandmas the picture never once fell. That apparently is the proper order of things.

The Cane

Grandpa lived with his daughter's family. He had a room upstairs, over the kitchen. His three grandchildren loved him very much. Each would try to stop in to visit him each day. He was usually sitting in his recliner with his cane on his lap. He always had the aroma of Old Spice aftershave. They would sit across from him and talk or play a game of cards.

He used a cane to walk but the last couple of years there were days his legs hurt and he preferred not coming down. Instead he would tap on his floor three times when he wanted something. In the kitchen someone would hear the three taps and go up and see what grandpa needed.

It was a sad day when he passed away. The grandchildren especially missed him. His room was kept pretty much as he had left it. Occasionally they would peek in, almost expecting him to be sitting there in his favorite chair with his cane on his lap. If they took a deep breath, they could still faintly smell his aftershave.

Several months after grandpa passed away, the three grandchildren were sitting at the kitchen table, reminiscing about him. As they drank coffee and talked there came three loud taps from the ceiling.

They looked at each other, and then raced upstairs. Opening the door, they could smell grandpa's aftershave as if he had just put it on. Lying across his recliner was his cane; they had put it away in the closet after he passed away.

Can't we all Just get Along?

Grandma was a dear soul and hated to hear her family argue. Whenever she was around, and they argued she would put a quick stop to it.

Grandma passed away several years ago. Her daughter's family moved to a home on Watson Road in Fairport. They hung grandma's picture in the hall.

Ever since the photo of grandma was hung up, a strange thing began to happen. Almost every time the family began to argue, grandma's picture would fall off the wall, loud enough for all to hear. In her way grandma still puts a quick end to arguments.

Waving Goodbye

Granddad had a wonderful garden; he loved growing flowers and vegetables. The family would visit every Sunday, and he and grandma would be out in the garden. They would pull in behind their parents green Chevrolet sedan and honk the horn, and their grandparents would look up, smile, and wave hello. Even from a distance, there was no mistaking granddad; he had his own distinctive manner of waving.

Granddad passed away, and grandma would go to visit his grave at Holy Sepulcher cemetery every Sunday. One day she had brought several of his favorite flowers to plant at the base of his headstone. She began talking to her husband; her eyes teared up as she told him how much she loved him. She dug the soil to plant the flowers.

The cemetery was silent and she was alone. Grandma told him how much she missed seeing him wave. From nowhere a green car drove past. She looked up, the car seemed blurred. But the driver was familiar, an older man who smiled and waved as he drove past -- yes it was that unique wave of granddad's! Then, in the blink of an eye the car and driver disappeared.

Watch Over Me

Talk to most nurses who work in any hospital and they will tell you of times when strange things happened at work. This story took place at Strong Memorial Hospital, one of Rochester's finest hospitals. Interestingly enough it sits across from Mount Hope Cemetery. Perhaps, not the most cheerful view for patients on that side of the hospital.

Pete was an EMT. He was on night duty when he got the call that his son, Jake was taken to Strong Memorial Hospital with a severe asthma attack. After notifying his ambulance headquarters he headed straight for the hospital.

When he got there, his son was in emergency. He told him how sorry he was that he could not get there sooner. Jake smiled and said, "Its ok dad, grandma was here keeping me company. She told me everything would be alright."

Pete looked at him and asked where she was. Jake said "Grandma told me she had to go but that you would be here in a minute."

Pete said "That was nice of mom's parents to come over right away." His son said "No dad, it was your mom." Pete looked at his son curiously, and said "Ok."

A few hours later Jake was released from the hospital; Pete took his son home. When they got there, Jake went to a picture of his grandmother and her second husband that was on the wall. He pointed to it and said "They both were there at the hospital, grandma did the talking. They looked just as they do here in this picture."

A strange feeling came over Pete as he looked at the picture of his mom and her second husband. They had both died years ago, before Jake was born.

113 - Ghosts of Old Rochesterville

Doing the Dishes

Joan's husband had passed away months ago. They loved each other dearly and she misses him terribly still feeling very distressed after his passing.

One of the endearing little things he would do after dinner when she was washing the dishes was to come up behind her and put his hands on her shoulders. She loved the feeling of his warm strong hands gently touching her.

Several months after he had passed away she was standing at the sink doing her dinner dishes when she felt warm hands on her shoulders just like she used to. At first it startled her. She thought she was just imagining it. Joan could feel each warm finger on her shoulders; they felt real; they were his hands. This has continued about every week or two. Joan believes it's her husband coming back to reassure her, and, since his visits, she has felt much better.

Of course she still misses him dearly but knows they will be reunited again. In the mean time she enjoys his spirited company when he stops by to keep in touch.

Ghostly Milk Trucks

Phantom Tanker

Years ago, late on a cold snowy night, a milk tanker was trying to make up for lost time due to the severe snow on routes 5 & 20. He was hauling 5000 gallons of milk, going faster than was prudent for the weather. As he passed the occasional car or truck, in their rear view mirror they would see his headlights grow in the blinding snow, and then a flash of his purple cab and silver tank as he roared passed them into the tempest. On one of the curves between Geneva and Bloomfield, his rig began to slide sideways as he hit the curve. Smashing through the guard rail the truck rolled on its side. By the time help arrived, it was too late for the driver.

In 2006, Jim began to drive a newspaper delivery truck along 5 & 20. Jim remembers one very cold and snowy February night well. He was a few miles past Geneva when he saw a pair of headlights in his rear view mirror. They were coming up fast. An odd chill went through him. The headlights swung out in the passing lane. Jim glimpsed an older purple cab hauling a stainless tank, a milk tanker. It zoomed passed him, and, just as it pulled ahead, it disappeared. He could see only the driving snow flakes lit up by his headlights.

If you travel route 5 & 20 between Geneva and Bloomfield, late, on a dark and cold winter night, you may see the phantom milk truck. It's headlights in the mirror roaring up from behind and passing you in the left lane. Feel a cold chill as the phantom passes you and vanishes into the icy swirls, racing to make a delivery long past due.

The Old Milk Wagon

In the 1960's, Andrea lived with her family near Silver Stadium, the old Ball Park in Rochester. Her brother, Tom worked for Kodak and rose before dawn for work. As he left the house each morning he would pause and listen.

Out of the predawn darkness came the sound of iron horse shoes on the pavement. It was a sound that had not been heard for thirty or forty years in that area. Cars and trucks had long since replaced horse drawn wagons and carriages.

He would wait as the apparition of an old milk wagon pulled along by horse passed by the house. The mare's iron shoes made a slow "clop, clop" sound as they passed the house. For a moment it was surreal, listening to the horse, and catching a glimpse of the milk wagon as it went by. It was like going back in time. As the sounds of the horse and wagon faded the spell was broken and he would start off for work.

Andrea always heard Tom get ready for work. She would listen at her window for the door, and then, the slow "clop, clop" of the ghostly milk man's horse. With that sound, she would smile, knowing her brother was off to work.

Bathroom Boos

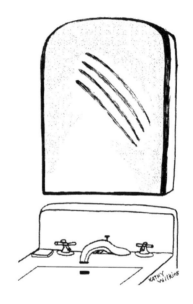

Just when you thought it was safe to take a shower again…

Doreen is a waitress I met a few years ago at a local restaurant. Over the years I would run into her now and then and we would catch up. The last time I saw her she told me about a strange incident that happened to her in her apartment. Doreen lived in an average upstairs apartment with her 2 children near Culver Road.

She was running the hot water for her shower and she went to check on her children. They were sleeping soundly in their room.

When she went back in the bathroom, the air was warm and steamy, the mirror misted over. She disrobed and went in the shower. The hot water felt wonderful after the day she had at work.

Finishing, she opened the shower curtain and looked at the mirror. A feeling of horror swept over her. What looked like a four clawed hand had streaked its mark across the mirror in the warm mist.

Heart racing, she grabbed her robe and ran out of the bathroom to check on her children. They were still sleeping peacefully in their room. The apartment door was bolted. Her heart was still pounding; she went to the kitchen, grabbed a heavy cast iron frying pan and searched the small apartment to be sure no one was hiding.

From that time on she always felt like someone was watching when she was in the bathroom, especially when she took a shower. Several months later she moved to another apartment with a private bath.

Peeping Tom

Up in Seabreeze NY, is the firehouse. There are many stories about the ghosts in the firehouse from children to the first chief of the fire department. This one always takes place in the second floor ladies room.

The second floor has a meeting hall, kitchen, and, of course, bathrooms. Over the years, a several women have reported seeing a pair of eyes watching them from the bathroom mirror in the ladies room.

Knock, Knock

The Reunion Inn on Culver Road was built as a private residence by Captain Samuel and Lavinia Bradstreet in 1856; it has quite a history. It was a stop on the Underground Railroad, became a speakeasy during prohibition, and has quite a few ghost stories attached to it. This one takes place in the upstairs bathroom.

One of the waitresses who had refused to believe any of the ghost stories she had heard about the Reunion over the years, went to the upstairs bathroom as she always had done. The upstairs one had been remodeled and was nicer than the downstairs ladies room. It's one of those girl things; while men are content to find the nearest tree, women like a pleasant restroom.

She was taking care of business when suddenly there was a knock on the door. She was surprised, as she had seen no one else up there when she had come in.

She said "I'll be right out." A few seconds later another knock. Again she said "I'll be right out." There was no reply just another knock on the door.

Well the waitress became a bit annoyed and thought it might be one of the staff playing a joke on her. Figuring she would surprise whoever was knocking, she quietly went to the door and waited. The knocking began again; she quickly pushed the door open with her body. She nearly fell down as the door swung open freely.

There was no one in front of the door; she looked behind it – no one there either. She searched the upstairs and there was nobody around, well nobody she could see. It was the last time she went to the upstairs bathroom at the Reunion.

Hazards of Remodeling

Both Kate and her cat had not been happy in her last house. Kate really wanted a smaller house, one that her cat would be content in also. Kitty it seems was always looking up and hissing then leaving the room, as if there was something there that she didn't like in the house.

Kate went to look at an older house on Cinnabar Road. in Rochester. A feeling of welcome had overcome her when she when she first walked in the front door; consequently, she felt it was the right house for her. She even brought her kitty to approve the home. The cat walked around the rooms then plopped herself down in the living room and began to purr. Kate put the purchase offer in that day.

Now Kate is a bit sensitive to spirits, and, when she moved in, she began to feel the presence of a woman there. She knew that this woman was making her feel welcome in the home. The new house seemed perfect, Kate was very comfortable with the ghost, and the cat was relaxed and quite happy here.

Kate, her cat, and the ghost got along well at first. She could always tell when the ghost didn't like a visitor; a creeping coldness would swallow up the room and only when the guest left would it feel warm again.

It was an older home and Kate wanted to do some remodeling, starting with the bathroom. Well the ghost was not pleased that the house was being remolded. Kate could feel her abhorrence for changing the house. Kate was determined to finish the work despite her noncorporeal housemate's objections.

One morning during the remodeling Kate was taking her shower when she felt two hands push her shoulders. She fell back on the shower curtain, tore it down and ended up in a most undignified position on her back with her knees and feet hanging over the inside edge of the tub.

It took her a moment to clear her head from the shock of falling. She laid there thinking about what happened then began carefully moving, making sure nothing was broken. As she began to untangle herself from the shower curtain and get up, she realized her head was on the floor where the edge of the commode should have been. She shivered with the thought of her head hitting the porcelain.

When she shakily stood up she could not believe her eyes. The commode had been moved, about six inches, just enough to clear her head as she fell. It appeared like someone had carefully picked the fixture up and placed it down in the new spot. No water spilled, the bolts and wax seal were still in the floor flange and water connection all undamaged.

The only explanation seemed to be that the ghost moved it. The ghost didn't want to hurt Kate just get her message across. Kate continued to butt heads with the ghost during the remodeling but the spirit never tried to get pushy again and the remodeling proceeded.

She did get a very strange look from her contractor when she showed him the bathroom and asked him to set the commode back in its original place.

127 - Ghosts of Old Rochesterville